Rows 9 and 10: Repeat Rows 7 and 8: 102 sts and 45 chs.

Row 11: With **right** side facing, join Red with sc in first sc; ★ working in **front** of next ch, dc in skipped dc one row **below**, (sc in next sc, working in **front** of next ch, dc in skipped dc one row **below**) twice, sc in next 5 dc; repeat from ★ across to last 6 sts, (working in **front** of next ch, dc in skipped dc one row **below**, sc in next sc) 3 times; finish off: 147 sts.

Row 12: With **wrong** side facing, join Purple with sc in first sc; ★ ch 1, skip next st, sc in next sc; repeat from ★ across; finish off: 74 sc and 73 chs.

Row 13: With **right** side facing, join Red with sc in first sc; ★ working in **front** of next ch, dc in skipped st one row **below**, sc in next sc; repeat from ★ across; finish off: 147 sts.

Rows 14-125: Repeat Rows 4-13, 11 times; then repeat Rows 4 and 5 once **more**.

TRIM
FIRST SIDE
Row 1: With **wrong** side facing, join Red with sc in first sc; ★ ch 1, skip next dc, sc in next sc; repeat from ★ across; finish off: 74 sc and 73 ch-1 sps.

Row 2: With **right** side facing, join Red with slip st in first sc; (slip st in next ch-1 sp, ch 1) across to last ch-1 sp, slip st in last ch-1 sp and in last sc; finish off.

SECOND SIDE
Row 1: With **wrong** side facing and working in free loops of beginning ch *(Fig. 2b, page 25)*, join Red with sc in first ch at base of first sc; ★ ch 1, skip next ch, sc in next ch; repeat from ★ across; finish off: 74 sc and 73 ch-1 sps.

Row 2: With **right** side facing, join Red with slip st in first sc; (slip st in next ch-1 sp, ch 1) across to last ch-1 sp, slip st in last ch-1 sp and in last sc; finish off.

Using photo as a guide for placement and one strand of corresponding color yarn, 11½" (29 cm) long, add additional fringe in each row across short edges of Lap Robe *(Figs. 5a & b, page 26)*.

SLIPPERS
■■■□ INTERMEDIATE

Finished Sole Length:
Small	Medium	Large
9" (23 cm)	9½" (24 cm)	10" (25.5 cm)

Size Note: Yarn amounts and gauge are given for size Small with sizes Medium and Large in braces { }. Follow the same instructions for **all** sizes. Finished measurement is obtained by using a different hook size as recommended in Materials.

MATERIALS
Medium/Worsted Weight Yarn (4) MEDIUM
 [3½ ounces, 198 yards
   (100 grams, 181 meters) per skein]:
 Purple - 1 skein
   [8 ounces, 452 yards
     (226 grams, 415 meters) per skein]:
 Red - 1 skein
Crochet hook as indicated below **or** size needed for gauge
  Size Small: size G (4 mm)
  Size Medium: size H (5 mm)
  Size Large: size I (5.5 mm)
Safety pin
Marker
Yarn needle

GAUGE: In pattern, 15{14-13} sts and 16{15-14} rows = 4" (10 cm)

Gauge Swatch: 4" (10 cm) square
With Red, ch 16{15-14}.
Row 1: Sc in second ch from hook and in each ch across: 15{14-13} sts.
Rows 2 thru 16{15-14}: Ch 1, turn; sc in each sc across.
Finish off.

Inst

STITCH GUIDE

RIGHT DECREASE (uses next 2 sts)
Pull up a loop in next sc, YO, working **behind** next ch, insert hook in skipped st one rnd **below**, YO and pull up a loop, YO and draw through 2 loops on hook, YO and draw through all 3 loops on hook.

LEFT DECREASE (uses next 2 sts)
YO, working **behind** next ch, insert hook in skipped st one rnd **below**, YO and pull up a loop, YO and draw through 2 loops on hook, pull up a loop in next sc, YO and draw through all 3 loops on hook.

SOLE

With Red, ch 24.

Rnd 1 (Right side): 2 Sc in second ch from hook, sc in next 9 chs, hdc in next 3 chs, dc in next 7 chs, 2 dc in next ch, hdc in next ch, 5 sc in last ch (toe); working in free loops of beginning ch *(Fig. 2b, page 25)*, hdc in next ch, 2 dc in next ch, dc in next 7 chs, hdc in next 3 chs, sc in next 9 chs, 2 sc in same ch as first sc; do **not** join, place marker *(see Markers, page 24)*: 53 sts.

Note: Loop a short piece of yarn around any stitch to mark Rnd 1 as **right** side.

Rnd 2: 2 Sc in each of next 2 sc, sc in next 22 sts, 2 sc in next sc, (sc in next sc, 2 sc in next sc) twice, sc in next 22 sts, 2 sc in each of next 2 sc: 60 sc.

Rnd 3: Sc in next sc, 2 sc in next sc, sc in next 23 sc, 2 sc in next sc, (sc in next 2 sc, 2 sc in next sc) 3 times, sc in next 23 sc, 2 sc in next sc, sc in next sc: 66 sc.

Rnd 4: Sc in next sc, 2 sc in next sc, sc in next 26 sc, 2 sc in next sc, (sc in next 2 sc, 2 sc in next sc) 3 times, sc in next 26 sc, 2 sc in next sc, sc in next sc: 72 sc.

Rnd 5: Sc in next 33 sc, 2 sc in next sc, sc in next 4 sc, 2 sc in next sc, sc in next 33 sc; do **not** finish off: 74 sc.

SIDES

Rnd 1: Sc in each sc around; slip st in next sc to join, remove marker and place loop from hook onto safety pin to keep piece from unraveling as you work the next rnd.

Always keep safety pin and working yarn on **wrong** side of work.

Rnd 2: With **wrong** side facing, join Purple with sc in sc before joining *(see Joining With Sc, page 25)*; ch 1, skip next sc, ★ sc in next sc, ch 1, skip next sc; repeat from ★ around; join with slip st to first sc, finish off: 37 sc and 37 chs.

Rnd 3: With **right** side facing, remove safety pin and place Red loop onto loop; ch 3 **(counts as first dc, now and throughout)**, sc in next sc, ★ working **behind** next ch *(Fig. 3, page 25)*, dc in skipped sc one rnd **below**, sc in next sc; repeat from ★ around; join with slip st to first dc, place loop from hook onto safety pin to keep piece from unraveling as you work the next rnd: 74 sts.

Rnd 4: With **wrong** side facing, join Purple with sc in sc before joining; ch 1, skip next dc, ★ sc in next sc, ch 1, skip next st; repeat from ★ around; join with slip st to first sc, finish off: 37 sc and 37 chs.

Rnd 5: With **right** side facing, remove safety pin and place Red loop onto hook; ch 3, (sc in next sc, working **behind** next ch, dc in skipped dc one rnd **below**) 13 times, (sc in next sc, work Left decrease, working **behind** next ch, dc in skipped dc one rnd **below**) 3 times, work Right decrease, sc in next sc, (working **behind** next ch, dc in skipped dc one rnd **below**, work Right decrease, sc in next sc) twice, (working **behind** next ch, dc in skipped dc one rnd **below**, sc in next sc) 12 times; join with slip st to first dc, place loop from hook onto safety pin to keep piece from unraveling as you work the next rnd: 68 sts.

Rnd 6: Repeat Rnd 4: 34 sc and 34 chs.

Instructions continued on page 5.

1

Rnd 7: With **right** side facing, remove safety pin and place Red loop onto hook; ch 3, (sc in next sc, working **behind** next ch, dc in skipped dc one rnd **below**) 12 times, work Right decrease, sc in next sc, (working **behind** next ch, dc in skipped st one rnd **below**, work Right decrease, sc in next sc) twice, work Left decrease, (working **behind** next ch, dc in skipped st one rnd **below**, sc in next sc, work Left decrease) twice, (working **behind** next ch, dc in skipped dc one rnd **below**, sc in next sc) 11 times; join with slip st to first dc, place loop from hook onto safety pin to keep piece from unraveling as you work the next rnd: 62 sts.

Rnd 8: Repeat Rnd 4: 31 sc and 31 chs.

Rnd 9: With **right** side facing, remove safety pin and place Red loop onto hook; ch 3, (sc in next sc, working **behind** next ch, dc in skipped dc one rnd **below**) 9 times, place marker in last dc made for st placement, sc in next sc, (working **behind** next ch, dc in skipped st one rnd **below**, sc in next sc) 3 times, work Left decrease, working **behind** next ch, dc in skipped st one rnd **below**, sc in next sc, work Left decrease, (working **behind** next ch, dc in skipped st one rnd **below**, work Right decrease, sc in next sc) twice, (working **behind** next ch, dc in skipped dc one rnd **below**, sc in next sc) 11 times; join with slip st to first dc, place loop from hook onto safety pin to keep piece from unraveling as you work the Instep: 58 sts.

INSTEP

With **right** side facing, join Red with dc in marked dc *(see Joining With Dc, page 25)*; remove marker, dc in next 3 sts, hdc in next 4 sts, sc in next 3 sts, slip st in next 3 sts, sc in next 3 sts, hdc in next 4 sts, dc in next 4 sts, leave remaining 33 sts unworked; finish off leaving a long end for sewing: 25 sts.

With **right** side facing and using long end, whipstitch Instep sts together through **inside** loops only *(Fig. 4b, page 25)*, beginning in first dc and last dc and ending in center slip st.

CUFF

Rnd 1: With **right** side facing, remove safety pin and place Red loop onto hook; ch 1, sc in same st and in next 17 sts, dc in same dc as first dc of Instep; working in end of rows on Instep, sc around post of first dc, sc in next joining and around post of next dc, dc in same dc as last dc of Instep; sc in last 15 sts; join with slip st to first sc: 38 sts.

Rnd 2: Slip st loosely in next sc and in each st around; join with slip st to joining slip st, finish off.

2. DESERT SUNSET SLIPPERS & THROW
Shown on page 8.

LAP ROBE
■■□□ EASY

Finished Size: 36" x 51" (91.5 cm x 129.5 cm)

MATERIALS
Medium/Worsted Weight Yarn [MEDIUM 4]
[$3^1/2$ ounces, 198 yards
(100 grams, 181 meters) per skein]:
White - 2 skeins
Yellow - 2 skeins
Orange - 2 skeins
Red - 2 skeins
Purple - 2 skeins
Blue - 2 skeins
Green - 2 skeins
Crochet hook, size H (5 mm) **or** size needed for gauge

GAUGE: In pattern,
15 sts and 16 rows = 4" (10 cm)

Gauge Swatch: 4" (10 cm) square
With White, ch 16.
Work same as Afghan Body for 16 rows.

STRIPE SEQUENCE
2 Rows **each**: White, ★ Yellow, Orange, Red, Purple, Blue, Green, White; repeat from ★ for sequence.

Each row is worked across length of Lap Robe. When joining yarn and finishing off, leave a $5^1/2$" (14 cm) end to be worked into fringe.

BODY
With White, ch 192.

Row 1 (Right side): Sc in second ch from hook, ★ ch 1, skip next ch, sc in next ch; repeat from ★ across; finish off: 96 sc and 95 ch-1 sps.

Note: Loop a short piece of yarn around any stitch to mark Row 1 as **right** side.

Row 2: With **wrong** side facing, join White with sc in first sc *(see Joining With Sc, page 25)*; (ch 1, sc in next sc) across; finish off.

Row 3: With **right** side facing, join next color with sc in first sc; (ch 1, sc in next sc) across; finish off.

Row 4: With **wrong** side facing, join same color with sc in first sc; (ch 1, sc in next sc) across; finish off.

Repeat Rows 3 and 4 in Stripe Sequence until Body measures approximately $35^1/2$" (90 cm) from beginning ch, ending by working 2 rows of White.

TRIM
FIRST SIDE
With **right** side facing, join White with slip st in first sc on last row; (slip st in next ch-1 sp, ch 1) across to last ch-1 sp, slip st in last ch-1 sp and in last sc; finish off.

SECOND SIDE
With **right** side facing and working in sps and in free loops across beginning ch *(Fig. 2b, page 25)*, join White with slip st in first ch; (slip st in next sp, ch 1) across to last sp, slip st in last sp and in ch at base of last sc; finish off.

Using photo as a guide for placement and holding 2 strands of corresponding color yarn together, each $11^1/2$" (29 cm) long, add additional fringe in each row across short edges of Lap Robe *(Figs. 5a & b, page 26)*.

Instructions continued on page 7.

SLIPPERS
■■■□ INTERMEDIATE

Finished Sole Length:
Small	Medium	Large
9" (23 cm)	9½" (24 cm)	10" (25.5 cm)

Size Note: Yarn amounts and gauge are given for size Small with sizes Medium and Large in braces { }. Follow the same instructions for **all** sizes. Finished measurement is obtained by using a different hook size as recommended in Materials.

MATERIALS
Medium/Worsted Weight Yarn [MEDIUM 4]
  [3½ ounces, 198 yards
    (100 grams, 181 meters) per skein]:
  Yellow - 1 skein
  Blue - 60 yards (55 meters)
  Red - 60 yards (55 meters)
  Green - 60 yards (55 meters)
  Orange - 30 yards (27.5 meters)
  Purple - 30 yards (27.5 meters)
Crochet hook as indicated below **or** size needed for gauge
  Size Small: size G (4 mm)
  Size Medium: size H (5 mm)
  Size Large: size I (5.5 mm)
Safety pin
Marker
Yarn needle

GAUGE: In pattern, 15{14-13} sts and 16{15-14} rows = 4" (10 cm)

Gauge Swatch: 4" (10 cm) square
With Yellow, ch 16{15-14}.
Row 1: Sc in second ch from hook and in each ch across: 15{14-13} sc.
Rows 2 thru 16{15-14}: Ch 1, turn; sc in each sc across.
Finish off.

STITCH GUIDE

RIGHT DECREASE (uses next 2 sts)
Pull up a loop in next sc, YO, working **behind** next ch, insert hook in skipped st one rnd **below**, YO and pull up a loop, YO and draw through 2 loops on hook, YO and draw through all 3 loops on hook.

LEFT DECREASE (uses next 2 sts)
YO, working **behind** next ch, insert hook in skipped st one rnd **below**, YO and pull up a loop, YO and draw through 2 loops on hook, pull up a loop in next sc, YO and draw through all 3 loops on hook.

SOLE
With Yellow, ch 24.

Rnd 1 (Right side)**:** 2 Sc in second ch from hook, sc in next 9 chs, hdc in next 3 chs, dc in next 7 chs, 2 dc in next ch, hdc in next ch, 5 sc in last ch (toe); working in free loops of beginning ch *(Fig. 2b, page 25)*, hdc in next ch, 2 dc in next ch, dc in next 7 chs, hdc in next 3 chs, sc in next 9 chs, 2 sc in same ch as first sc; do **not** join, place marker *(see Markers, page 24)*: 53 sts.

Note: Loop a short piece of yarn around any stitch to mark Rnd 1 as **right** side.

Rnd 2: 2 Sc in each of next 2 sc, sc in next 22 sts, 2 sc in next sc, (sc in next sc, 2 sc in next sc) twice, sc in next 22 sts, 2 sc in each of next 2 sc: 60 sc.

Rnd 3: Sc in next sc, 2 sc in next sc, sc in next 23 sc, 2 sc in next sc, (sc in next 2 sc, 2 sc in next sc) 3 times, sc in next 23 sc, 2 sc in next sc, sc in next sc: 66 sc.

Rnd 4: Sc in next sc, 2 sc in next sc, sc in next 26 sc, 2 sc in next sc, (sc in next 2 sc, 2 sc in next sc) 3 times, sc in next 26 sc, 2 sc in next sc, sc in next sc: 72 sc.

Rnd 5: Sc in next 33 sc, 2 sc in next sc, sc in next 4 sc, 2 sc in next sc, sc in next 33 sc; do **not** finish off: 74 sc.

Instructions continued on page 9.

2

SIDES

Rnd 1: Sc in each sc around; slip st in next sc to join, remove marker and place loop from hook onto safety pin to keep piece from unraveling as you work the next rnd.

Always keep safety pin and working yarn on **wrong** side of work.

Rnd 2: With **wrong** side facing, join Green with sc in sc before joining *(see Joining With Sc, page 25)*; ch 1, skip next sc, ★ sc in next sc, ch 1, skip next sc; repeat from ★ around; join with slip st to first sc, finish off: 37 sc and 37 chs.

Rnd 3: With **right** side facing, remove safety pin and place Yellow loop onto hook; ch 3 **(counts as first dc, now and throughout)**, sc in next sc, ★ working **behind** next ch *(Fig. 3, page 25)*, dc in skipped sc one rnd **below**, sc in next sc; repeat from ★ around; join with slip st to first dc, place loop from hook onto safety pin to keep piece from unraveling as you work the next rnd: 74 sts.

Rnd 4: With **wrong** side facing, join Blue with sc in sc before joining; ch 1, skip next dc, ★ sc in next st, ch 1, skip next st; repeat from ★ around; join with slip st to first sc, finish off: 37 sc and 37 chs.

Rnd 5: With **right** side facing, remove safety pin and place Yellow loop onto hook; ch 3, (sc in next sc, working **behind** next ch, dc in skipped dc one rnd **below**) 13 times, (sc in next sc, work Left decrease, working **behind** next ch, dc in skipped dc one rnd **below**) 3 times, work Right decrease, sc in next sc, (working **behind** next ch, dc in skipped dc one rnd **below**, work Right decrease, sc in next sc) twice, (working **behind** next ch, dc in skipped dc one rnd **below**, sc in next sc) 12 times; join with slip st to first dc, place loop from hook onto safety pin to keep piece from unraveling as you work the next rnd: 68 sts.

Rnd 6: With Purple, repeat Rnd 4: 34 sc and 34 chs.

Rnd 7: With **right** side facing, remove safety pin and place Yellow loop onto hook; ch 3, (sc in next sc, working **behind** next ch, dc in skipped dc one rnd **below**) 12 times, work Right decrease, sc in next sc, (working **behind** next ch, dc in skipped st one rnd **below**, work Right decrease, sc in next sc) twice, work Left decrease, (working **behind** next ch, dc in skipped st one rnd **below**, sc in next sc, work Left decrease) twice, (working **behind** next ch, dc in skipped dc one rnd **below**, sc in next sc) 11 times; join with slip st to first dc, place loop from hook onto safety pin to keep piece from unraveling as you work the next rnd: 62 sts.

Rnd 8: With Red, repeat Rnd 4: 31 sc and 31 chs.

Rnd 9: With **right** side facing, remove safety pin and place Yellow loop onto hook; ch 3, (sc in next sc, working **behind** next ch, dc in skipped dc one rnd **below**) 9 times, place marker in last dc made for st placement, sc in next sc, (working **behind** next ch, dc in skipped dc one rnd **below**, sc in next sc) 3 times, work Left decrease, working **behind** next ch, dc in skipped st one rnd **below**, sc in next sc, work Left decrease, (working **behind** next ch, dc in skipped st one rnd **below**, work Right decrease, sc in next sc) twice, (working **behind** next ch, dc in skipped dc one rnd **below**, sc in next sc) 11 times; join with slip st to first dc, place loop from hook onto safety pin to keep piece from unraveling as you work the Instep and Rnd 1 of Cuff: 58 sts.

INSTEP

With **right** side facing, join Red with dc in marked dc *(see Joining With Dc, page 25)*; remove marker, dc in next 3 sts, hdc in next 4 sts, sc in next 3 sts, slip st in next 3 sts, sc in next 3 sts, hdc in next 4 sts, dc in next 4 sts, leave remaining 33 sts unworked; finish off leaving a long end for sewing: 25 sts.

With **right** side facing and using long end, whipstitch Instep sts together through **inside** loops only *(Fig. 4b, page 25)*, beginning in first dc and last dc and ending in center slip st.

CUFF

Rnd 1: With **wrong** side facing, join Orange with sc in sc before joining on Rnd 9 of Sides; ch 1, (skip next dc, sc in next sc, ch 1) 8 times, (sc around post of **next** dc of Instep, ch 1) twice, (sc in next sc, ch 1, skip next dc) 8 times; join with slip st to first sc, finish off: 19 sc and 19 chs.

Rnd 2: With **right** side facing, remove safety pin and place Yellow loop onto hook; ch 3, sc in next sc, (working **behind** next ch, dc in skipped dc one rnd **below**, sc in next sc) 8 times, working **behind** next ch, dc in same dc as first dc of Instep (on Rnd 9 of Sides), sc in next sc, working **behind** next ch, dc in Instep seam one rnd **below**, sc in next sc, working **behind** next ch, dc in same dc as last dc of Instep (on Rnd 9 of Sides), sc in next sc, (working **behind** next ch, dc in skipped dc one rnd **below**, sc in next sc) 7 times; join with slip st to first dc, place loop from hook onto safety pin to keep piece from unraveling as you work the next rnd: 38 sts.

Rnd 3: With **wrong** side facing, join a second strand of Yellow with sc in sc before joining; ch 1, skip next dc, ★ sc in next sc, ch 1, skip next dc; repeat from ★ around; join with slip st to first sc, finish off: 19 sc and 19 chs.

Rnd 4: With **right** side facing, remove safety pin and place Yellow loop onto hook; ch 3, sc in next sc, ★ working **behind** next ch, dc in skipped dc one rnd **below**, sc in next sc; repeat from ★ around; join with slip st to first dc: 38 sts.

Rnd 5: Slip st loosely in next sc and in each st around; join with slip st to joining slip st, finish off.

RUFFLES
SIDES

With **right** side facing, Sole toward you, and starting on Rnd 2 of Sides, join Green with slip st in Back Loop Only of ch at center of heel *(Fig. 1, page 25)*; ch 7, slip st in Front Loop Only of same ch, ch 7, ★ slip st in Back Loop Only of next ch, ch 7, slip st in Front Loop Only of same ch, ch 7; repeat from ★ around; join with slip st to **both** loops of joining slip st, finish off.

With corresponding color, repeat on Rnds 4, 6, and 8 of Sides.

INSTEP

Working in free loops of sts on Instep *(Fig. 2a, page 25)*, join Red with slip st in first dc; (ch 7, slip st in next st) around; finish off.

CUFF

With corresponding color and working in same manner as Sides, work Ruffles on Rnds 1 and 3 of Cuff.

3. DREAMY SLIPPERS & THROW
Shown on Front Cover.

LAP ROBE
■■■□ INTERMEDIATE

Finished Size: 32 1/2" x 46"
(82.5 cm x 117 cm)

MATERIALS
Medium/Worsted Weight Yarn [MEDIUM 4]
[5 ounces, 302 yards
(140 grams, 276 meters) per skein]:
Pink - 4 skeins
Green - 2 skeins
Crochet hook, size H (5 mm) **or** size needed for gauge
Safety pin
Yarn needle

GAUGE SWATCH: 4 1/2" (11.5 cm) square
Work same as Square.

STITCH GUIDE

BEGINNING CLUSTER (uses one st)
Ch 2, ★ YO, insert hook in same st, YO and pull up a loop, YO and draw through 2 loops on hook; repeat from ★ once **more**, YO and draw through all 3 loops on hook.

CLUSTER (uses one st)
★ YO, insert hook in st indicated, YO and pull up a loop, YO and draw through 2 loops on hook; repeat from ★ 2 times **more**, YO and draw through all 4 loops on hook.

DECREASE
Pull up a loop in next 2 sc, YO and draw through all 3 loops on hook.

SQUARE (Make 70)
Rnd 1 (Right side): With Green, ch 2, 8 sc in second ch from hook; join with slip st to first sc.

Note: Loop a short piece of yarn around any stitch to mark Rnd 1 as **right** side.

Rnd 2: Work Beginning Cluster, ch 3, (work Cluster in next sc, ch 3) around; join with slip st to top of Beginning Cluster, finish off: 8 Clusters and 8 ch-3 sps.

Rnd 3: With **right** side facing, join Pink with sc in any ch-3 sp *(see Joining With Sc, page 25)*; 2 sc in same sp, 5 sc in each of next 7 ch-3 sps, 2 sc in same sp as first sc; join with slip st to first sc: 40 sc.

Rnd 4: Ch 1, sc in same st, ★ † hdc in next sc, dc in next sc, ch 3, dc in next sc, hdc in next sc, sc in next 2 sc, decrease †, sc in next 2 sc; repeat from ★ 2 times **more**, then repeat from † to † once, sc in last sc; join with slip st to first sc; place loop from hook onto safety pin to keep piece from unraveling as you work the next rnd: 36 sts and 4 ch-3 sps.

Rnd 5: With **wrong** side facing and keeping safety pin and working yarn on **wrong** side of work, join Green with sc in any corner ch-3 sp; ch 2, sc in same sp, ★ † ch 1, skip next dc, (sc in next st, ch 1, skip next st) 4 times †, (sc, ch 2, sc) in next corner ch-3 sp; repeat from ★ 2 times **more**, then repeat from † to † once; join with slip st to first sc, finish off: 24 sc and 24 sps.

Rnd 6: With **right** side facing, remove safety pin and place Pink loop onto hook; ch 3 (**counts as first dc**), sc in next sc, working **behind** next ch *(Fig. 3, page 25)*, dc in skipped dc one rnd **below**, sc in next sc, ★ † working **behind** next corner ch-2, (dc, ch 3, dc) in ch-3 sp one rnd **below** (between sc), sc in next sc †, (working **behind** next ch, dc in skipped st one rnd **below**, sc in next sc) 5 times; repeat from ★ 2 times **more**, then repeat from † to † once, (working **behind** next ch, dc in skipped st one rnd **below**, sc in next sc) 3 times; join with slip st to first dc, finish off: 52 sts and 4 ch-3 sps.

11

ASSEMBLY

With Pink and working through **both** loops, whipstitch Squares together *(Fig. 4a, page 25)*, forming 7 vertical strips of 10 Squares each, beginning in center ch of first corner ch-3 and ending in center ch of next corner ch-3; then whipstitch strips together in same manner.

EDGING

Rnd 1: With **right** side facing, join Pink with sc in any corner ch-3 sp; ★ † ch 1, skip next dc, (sc in next sc, ch 1, skip next dc) 6 times, [hdc in same sp as joining on same Square, ch 1, hdc in same sp as joining on next Square, ch 1, skip next dc, (sc in next sc, ch 1, skip next dc) 6 times] across to next corner ch-3 sp †, (sc, ch 2, sc) in next corner ch-3 sp; repeat from ★ 2 times **more**, then repeat from † to † once, sc in same sp as first sc, ch 1, sc in first sc to form last corner ch-2 sp: 272 sps.

Rnd 2: Ch 1, sc in last ch-2 sp made, ch 1, (sc in next ch-1 sp, ch 1) across to next corner ch-2 sp, ★ (sc, ch 2, sc) in corner ch-2 sp, ch 1, (sc in next ch-1 sp, ch 1) across to next corner ch-2 sp; repeat from ★ 2 times **more**, sc in same sp as first sc, hdc in first sc to form last corner ch-2 sp: 276 sps.

Rnd 3: (Slip st, ch 2, slip st) in last ch-2 sp made, ch 1, ★ (slip st in next ch-1 sp, ch 1) across to next corner ch-2 sp, (slip st, ch 2, slip st) in corner ch-2 sp; repeat from ★ 2 times **more**, (slip st in next ch-1 sp, ch 1) across; join with slip st to first slip st, finish off.

SLIPPERS

■■■□ INTERMEDIATE

Finished Sole Length:

Small	Medium	Large
9" (23 cm)	9½" (24 cm)	10" (25.5 cm)

Size Note: Yarn amounts and gauge are given for size Small with sizes Medium and Large in braces { }. Follow the same instructions for **all** sizes. Finished measurement is obtained by using a different hook size as recommended in Materials.

MATERIALS

MEDIUM (4)

Medium/Worsted Weight Yarn
  [5 ounces, 302 yards
    (140 grams, 276 meters) per skein]:
  Green - 1 skein
  Pink - 1 skein
Crochet hook as indicated below **or** size needed for gauge
  Size Small: size G (4 mm)
  Size Medium: size H (5 mm)
  Size Large: size I (5.5 mm)
Safety pin
Marker
Yarn needle

GAUGE: In pattern, 15{14-13} sts and 16{15-14} rows = 4" (10 cm)

Gauge Swatch: 4" (10 cm) square
With Green, ch 16{15-14}.
Row 1: Sc in second ch from hook and in each ch across: 15{14-13} sts.
Rows 2 thru 16{15-14}: Ch 1, turn; sc in each sc across.
Finish off.

Instructions begin on page 13.

STITCH GUIDE

RIGHT DECREASE (uses next 2 sts)
Pull up a loop in next sc, YO, working **behind** next ch, insert hook in skipped st one rnd **below**, YO and pull up a loop, YO and draw through 2 loops on hook, YO and draw through all 3 loops on hook.

LEFT DECREASE (uses next 2 sts)
YO, working **behind** next ch, insert hook in skipped st one rnd **below**, YO and pull up a loop, YO and draw through 2 loops on hook, pull up a loop in next sc, YO and draw through all 3 loops on hook.

SOLE

With Green, ch 24.

Rnd 1 (Right side)**:** 2 Sc in second ch from hook, sc in next 9 chs, hdc in next 3 chs, dc in next 7 chs, 2 dc in next ch, hdc in next ch, 5 sc in last ch (toe); working in free loops of beginning ch *(Fig. 2b, page 25)*, hdc in next ch, 2 dc in next ch, dc in next 7 chs, hdc in next 3 chs, sc in next 9 chs, 2 sc in same ch as first sc; do **not** join, place marker *(see Markers, page 24)*: 53 sts.

Note: Loop a short piece of yarn around any stitch to mark Rnd 1 as **right** side.

Rnd 2: 2 Sc in each of next 2 sc, sc in next 22 sts, 2 sc in next sc, (sc in next sc, 2 sc in next sc) twice, sc in next 22 sts, 2 sc in each of next 2 sc: 60 sc.

Rnd 3: Sc in next sc, 2 sc in next sc, sc in next 23 sc, 2 sc in next sc, (sc in next 2 sc, 2 sc in next sc) 3 times, sc in next 23 sc, 2 sc in next sc, sc in next sc: 66 sc.

Rnd 4: Sc in next sc, 2 sc in next sc, sc in next 26 sc, 2 sc in next sc, (sc in next 2 sc, 2 sc in next sc) 3 times, sc in next 26 sc, 2 sc in next sc, sc in next sc: 72 sc.

Rnd 5: Sc in next 33 sc, 2 sc in next sc, sc in next 4 sc, 2 sc in next sc, sc in next 33 sc; do **not** finish off: 74 sc.

SIDES

Rnd 1: Sc in each sc around; slip st in next sc to join, remove marker and place loop from hook onto safety pin to keep piece from unraveling as you work the next rnd.

Always keep safety pin and working yarn on **wrong** side of work.

Rnd 2: With **wrong** side facing, join Pink with sc in sc before joining *(see Joining With Sc, page 25)*; ch 1, skip next sc, ★ sc in next sc, ch 1, skip next sc; repeat from ★ around; join with slip st to first sc, finish off: 37 sc and 37 chs.

Rnd 3: With **right** side facing, remove safety pin and place Green loop onto hook; ch 3 **(counts as first dc, now and throughout)**, sc in next sc, ★ working **behind** next ch *(Fig. 3, page 25)*, dc in skipped sc one rnd **below**, sc in next sc; repeat from ★ around; join with slip st to first dc, place loop from hook onto safety pin to keep piece from unraveling as you work the next rnd.

Rnd 4: With **wrong** side facing, join Pink with sc in sc before joining; ch 1, skip next dc, ★ sc in next sc, ch 1, skip next dc; repeat from ★ around; join with slip st to first sc, finish off: 37 sc and 37 chs.

Rnd 5: With **right** side facing, remove safety pin and place Green loop onto hook; ch 3, (sc in next sc, working **behind** next ch, dc in skipped dc one rnd **below**) 13 times, (sc in next sc, work Left decrease, working **behind** next ch, dc in skipped dc one rnd **below**) 3 times, work Right decrease, sc in next sc, (working **behind** next ch, dc in skipped dc one rnd **below**, work Right decrease, sc in next sc) twice, (working **behind** next ch, dc in skipped dc one rnd **below**, sc in next sc) 12 times; join with slip st to first dc, place loop from hook onto safety pin to keep piece from unraveling as you work the next rnd: 68 sts.

Rnd 6: Repeat Rnd 4: 34 sc and 34 chs.

Rnd 7: With **right** side facing, remove safety pin and place Green loop onto hook; ch 3, (sc in next sc, working **behind** next ch, dc in skipped dc one rnd **below**) 12 times, work Right decrease, sc in next sc, (working **behind** next ch, dc in skipped st one rnd **below**, work Right decrease, sc in next sc) twice, work Left decrease, (working **behind** next ch, dc in skipped st one rnd **below**, sc in next sc, work Left decrease) twice, (working **behind** next ch, dc in skipped dc one rnd **below**, sc in next sc) 11 times; join with slip st to first dc, place loop from hook onto safety pin to keep piece from unraveling as you work the next rnd: 62 sts.

Rnd 8: Repeat Rnd 4: 31 sc and 31 chs.

Rnd 9: With **right** side facing, remove safety pin and place Green loop onto hook; ch 3, (sc in next sc, working **behind** next ch, dc in skipped dc one rnd **below**) 9 times, place marker in last dc made for st placement, sc in next sc, (working **behind** next ch, dc in skipped st one rnd **below**, sc in next sc) 3 times, work Left decrease, working **behind** next ch, dc in skipped st one rnd **below**, sc in next sc, work Left decrease, (working **behind** next ch, dc in skipped st one rnd **below**, work Right decrease, sc in next sc) twice, (working **behind** next ch, dc in skipped dc one rnd **below**, sc in next sc) 11 times; join with slip st to first dc, place loop from hook onto safety pin to keep piece from unraveling as you work the Instep and Rnd 1 of Cuff: 58 sts.

INSTEP

With **right** side facing, join Green with dc in marked dc *(see Joining With Dc, page 25)*; remove marker, dc in next 3 sts, hdc in next 4 sts, sc in next 3 sts, slip st in next 3 sts, sc in next 3 sts, hdc in next 4 sts, dc in next 4 sts, leave remaining 33 sts unworked; finish off leaving a long end for sewing: 25 sts.

With **right** side facing and using long end, whipstitch Instep sts together through **inside** loops only *(Fig. 4b, page 25)*, beginning in first dc and last dc and ending in center slip st.

CUFF

Rnd 1: With **wrong** side facing, join Pink with sc in sc before joining on Rnd 9 of Sides; ch 1, (skip next dc, sc in next sc, ch 1) 8 times, (sc around post of **next** dc of Instep, ch 1) twice, (sc in next sc, ch 1, skip next dc) 8 times; join with slip st to first sc, finish off: 19 sc and 19 chs.

Rnd 2: With **right** side facing, remove safety pin and place Green loop onto hook; ch 3, sc in next sc, (working **behind** next ch, dc in skipped st one rnd **below**, sc in next sc) 8 times, working **behind** next ch, dc in same dc as first dc of Instep (on Rnd 9 of Sides), sc in next sc, working **behind** next ch, dc in joining one rnd **below**, sc in next sc, working **behind** next ch, dc in same dc as last dc of Instep (on Rnd 9 of Sides), sc in next sc, (working **behind** next ch, dc in skipped st one rnd **below**, sc in next sc) 7 times; join with slip st to first dc, place loop from hook onto safety pin to keep piece from unraveling as you work the next rnd: 38 sts.

Rnd 3: With **wrong** side facing, join Pink with sc in sc before joining; ch 1, skip next dc, ★ sc in next sc, ch 1, skip next dc; repeat from ★ around; join with slip st to first sc, finish off: 19 sc and 19 chs.

Rnd 4: With **right** side facing, remove safety pin and place Green loop onto hook; ch 3, sc in next sc, (working **behind** next ch, dc in skipped dc one rnd **below**, sc in next sc) around; join with slip st to first dc: 38 sts.

Rnd 5: Slip st loosely in next sc and in each st around; join with slip st to joining slip st, finish off.

RUFFLES

With **right** side facing, Sole toward you, and starting on Rnd 1 of Cuff, join Pink with slip st in Back Loop Only of ch at center of heel *(Fig. 1, page 25)*; † ch 7, slip st in Front Loop Only of same ch, ch 7, ★ slip st in Back Loop Only of next ch, ch 7, slip st in Front Loop Only of same ch, ch 7; repeat from ★ around †; working on Rnd 3 of Cuff, slip st in Back Loop Only of ch above joining slip st, repeat from † to † once; join with slip st to **both** loops of first slip st on Rnd 3, finish off.

4. LEISURE TIME SLIPPERS & THROW

LAP ROBE
■■■□ INTERMEDIATE

Finished Size: 33" x 45" (84 cm x 114.5 cm)

MATERIALS
Medium/Worsted Weight Yarn [MEDIUM 4]
 [3½ ounces, 225 yards
   (100 grams, 206 meters) per skein]:
 Brown - 4 skeins
 Ecru - 3 skeins
 Blue - 1 skein
Crochet hook, size H (5 mm) **or** size needed for gauge
Yarn needle

GAUGE SWATCH: 4" (10 cm) square
Work same as Square.

STITCH GUIDE
CLUSTER
Ch 3, ★ YO, insert hook in third ch from hook, YO and pull up a loop, YO and draw through 2 loops on hook; repeat from ★ 2 times **more**, YO and draw through all 4 loops on hook. Push Cluster to **right** side.

SQUARE (Make 88)
Rnd 1 (Wrong side)**:** With Blue, ch 2, (sc, work Cluster, ch 1) 4 times in second ch from hook; join with slip st to first sc, finish off: 4 Clusters and 4 sc.

Note: Loop a short piece of yarn around **back** of any Cluster on Rnd 1 to mark **right** side.

Rnd 2: With **right** side facing, join Ecru with sc in any sc *(see Joining With Sc, page 25)*; working **behind** next Cluster *(Fig. 3, page 25)*, dc in same ch as sc (between sc), ★ (sc, ch 3, sc) in next sc, working **behind** next Cluster, dc in same ch as sc (between sc); repeat from ★ 2 times **more**, sc in same ch as first sc, dc in first sc to form last ch-3 sp: 4 ch-3 sps.

Rnd 3: Ch 3 **(counts as first dc, now and throughout)**, (2 dc, ch 3, 3 dc) in last ch-3 sp made, ch 1, ★ (3 dc, ch 3, 3 dc) in next ch-3 sp, ch 1; repeat from ★ 2 times **more**; join with slip st to first dc, finish off: 8 sps.

Rnd 4: With **right** side facing, join Brown with dc in any corner ch-3 sp *(see Joining With Dc, page 25)*; ch 3, 3 dc in same sp, ch 1, 3 dc in next ch-1 sp, ch 1, ★ (3 dc, ch 3, 3 dc) in next ch-3 sp, ch 1, 3 dc in next ch-1 sp, ch 1; repeat from ★ 2 times **more**, 2 dc in same sp as first dc; join with slip st to first dc, finish off: 36 dc and 12 sps.

ASSEMBLY
With Brown and working through **both** loops, whipstitch Squares together *(Fig. 4a, page 25)*, forming 8 vertical strips of 11 Squares each, beginning in center ch of first corner ch-3 and ending in center ch of next corner ch-3; then whipstitch strips together in same manner.

EDGING
Rnd 1: With **right** side facing, join Brown with sc in any corner ch-3 sp; ★ † ch 1, skip next dc, sc in next dc, ch 1, (sc in next ch-1 sp, ch 1, skip next dc, sc in next dc, ch 1) twice, [(sc in same sp as joining on same Square, ch 1, sc in same sp as joining on next Square, ch 1, skip next dc, sc in next dc, ch 1, (sc in next ch-1 sp, ch 1, skip next dc, sc in next dc, ch 1) twice] across to next corner ch-3 sp †, (sc, ch 2, sc) in corner ch-3 sp; repeat from ★ 2 times **more**, then repeat from † to † once, sc in same sp as first sc, hdc in first sc to form last corner ch-2 sp: 266 sps.

Rnd 2: Ch 1, (sc, ch 2, sc) in last ch-2 sp made, ch 1, (sc in next ch-1 sp, ch 1) across to next corner ch-2 sp, ★ (sc, ch 2, sc) in corner ch-2 sp, ch 1, (sc in next ch-1 sp, ch 1) across to next corner ch-2 sp; repeat from ★ 2 times **more**; join with slip st to first sc: 270 sps.

Instructions continued on page 17.

4

16

Rnd 3: (Slip st, ch 2, slip st) in first corner ch-2 sp, ch 1, ★ (slip st in next ch-1 sp, ch 1) across to next corner ch-2 sp, (slip st, ch 2, slip st) in corner ch-2 sp, ch 1; repeat from ★ 2 times **more**, (slip st in next ch-1 sp, ch 1) across; join with slip st to first slip st, finish off.

SLIPPERS
■□□□ BEGINNER

Finished Sole Length:

Small	Medium	Large
9" (23 cm)	9½" (24 cm)	10" (25.5 cm)

Size Note: Yarn amounts and gauge are given for size Small with sizes Medium and Large in braces { }. Follow the same instructions for **all** sizes. Finished measurement is obtained by using a different hook size as recommended in Materials.

MATERIALS
Medium/Worsted Weight Yarn (4 MEDIUM)
[3½ ounces, 225 yards
(100 grams, 206 meters) per skein]:
Blue - 1 skein
Ecru - 30 yards (27.5 meters) for Pom-pom
Crochet hook as indicated below **or** size needed
for gauge
Size Small: size G (4 mm)
Size Medium: size H (5 mm)
Size Large: size I (5.5 mm)
Safety pin
Marker
Yarn needle

GAUGE: In pattern, 15{14-13} sts and 16{15-14} rows = 4" (10 cm)

Gauge Swatch: 4" (10 cm) square
With Blue, ch 16{15-14}.
Row 1: Sc in second ch from hook and in each ch across: 15{14-13} sc.
Rows 2 thru 16{15-14}: Ch 1, turn; sc in each sc across.
Finish off.

STITCH GUIDE
DECREASE
Pull up a loop in next 2 sts, YO and draw through all 3 loops on hook **(counts as one sc)**.

SOLE
With Blue, ch 24.

Rnd 1 (Right side)**:** 2 Sc in second ch from hook, sc in next 9 chs, hdc in next 3 chs, dc in next 7 chs, 2 dc in next ch, hdc in next ch, 5 sc in last ch (toe); working in free loops of beginning ch *(Fig. 2b, page 25)*, hdc in next ch, 2 dc in next ch, dc in next 7 chs, hdc in next 3 chs, sc in next 9 chs, 2 sc in same ch as first sc; do **not** join, place marker *(see Markers, page 24)*: 53 sts.

Note: Loop a short piece of yarn around any stitch to mark Rnd 1 as **right** side.

Rnd 2: 2 Sc in each of next 2 sc, sc in next 22 sts, 2 sc in next sc, (sc in next sc, 2 sc in next sc) twice, sc in next 22 sts, 2 sc in each of next 2 sc: 60 sc.

Rnd 3: Sc in next sc, 2 sc in next sc, sc in next 23 sc, 2 sc in next sc, (sc in next 2 sc, 2 sc in next sc) 3 times, sc in next 23 sc, 2 sc in next sc, sc in next sc: 66 sc.

Rnd 4: Sc in next sc, 2 sc in next sc, sc in next 26 sc, 2 sc in next sc, (sc in next 2 sc, 2 sc in next sc) 3 times, sc in next 26 sc, 2 sc in next sc, sc in next sc: 72 sc.

Rnd 5: Sc in next 33 sc, 2 sc in next sc, sc in next 4 sc, 2 sc in next sc, sc in next 33 sc; do **not** finish off: 74 sc.

SIDES
Rnd 1: Sc in each sc around; slip st in next sc to join, remove marker.

Rnds 2-4: Ch 1, **turn**; sc in same st and in each sc around; join with slip st to first sc.

Rnd 5: Ch 1, turn; sc in same st and in next 26 sc, decrease, (sc in next 2 sc, decrease) twice, sc in next sc, decrease, (sc in next 2 sc, decrease) twice, sc in last 26 sc; join with slip st to first sc: 68 sc.

Rnd 6: Ch 1, turn; sc in same st and in each sc around; join with slip st to first sc.

Rnd 7: Ch 1, turn; sc in same st and in next 23 sc, decrease, (sc in next 2 sc, decrease) twice, sc in next sc, decrease, (sc in next 2 sc, decrease) twice, sc in last 23 sc; join with slip st to first sc: 62 sc.

Rnd 8: Ch 1, turn; sc in same st and in each sc around; join with slip st to first sc.

Rnd 9: Ch 1, turn; sc in same st and in next 17 sc, place marker in last sc made for st placement, sc in next 7 sc, decrease, sc in next 2 sc, decrease, sc in next sc, decrease, sc in next 2 sc, decrease, sc in last 24 sc; join with slip st to first sc, do **not** finish off; place loop from hook onto safety pin to keep piece from unraveling as you work the Instep: 58 sc.

INSTEP

With **right** side facing, join Blue with dc in marked sc *(see Joining With Dc, page 25)*; dc in next 3 sc, hdc in next 4 sc, sc in next 3 sc, slip st in next 3 sc, sc in next 3 sc, hdc in next 4 sc, dc in next 4 sc, leave remaining 33 sts unworked; finish off leaving a long end for sewing: 25 sts.

With **right** side facing and using long end, whipstitch Instep sts together through **both** loops *(Fig. 4a, page 25)*, beginning in first dc and last dc and ending in center slip st.

CUFF

Rnd 1: With **right** side facing, remove safety pin and place loop onto hook; ch 1, sc in same st and in next 16 sc, dc in same dc as first dc of Instep; working in end of rows on Instep, sc around post of first dc, sc in next joining and around post of next dc, dc in same dc as last dc of Instep; sc in last 16 sc; join with slip st to first sc: 38 sts.

Rnd 2: Slip st loosely in next sc and in each st around; join with slip st to joining slip st, finish off.

POM-POM (Make 2)

Cut a piece of cardboard 3" (7.5 cm) wide and 2¹/₂" (6.5 cm) wide.

Wind Ecru yarn around the cardboard until it is approximately ¹/₂" (12 mm) thick in the middle *(Fig. A)*.

Carefully slip the yarn off the cardboard and firmly tie an 18" (45.5 cm) length of yarn around the middle *(Fig. B)*. Leave yarn ends long enough to attach the pom-pom. Cut the loops on both ends and trim the pom-pom into a smooth ball *(Fig. C)*.

Fig. A

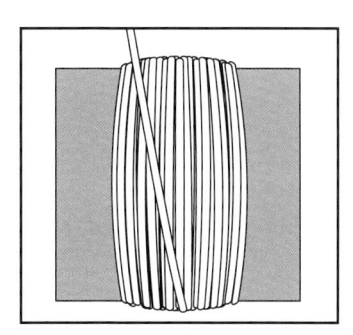

Fig. B

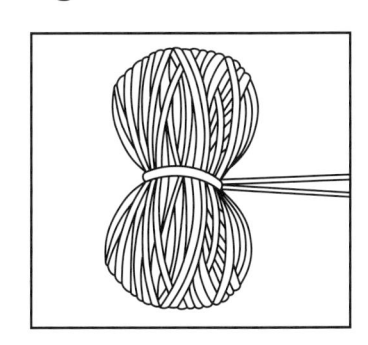

Fig. C

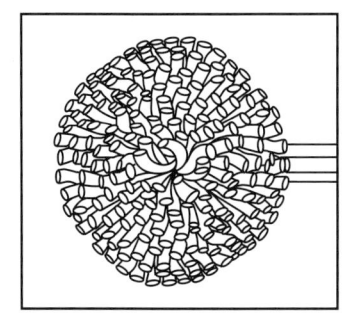

Using photo as a guide for placement, sew one Pom-pom to each slipper.

5. SOOTHING SLIPPERS & THROW

Shown on Back Cover.

LAP ROBE
■■■□ INTERMEDIATE

Finished Size: 35¹/₂" x 48" (90 cm x 122 cm)

MATERIALS
Medium/Worsted Weight Yarn (4 MEDIUM)
  [6 ounces, 330 yards
    (170 grams, 300 meters) per skein]:
  Red - 5 skeins
  Ecru - 1 skein
  Crochet hook, size H (5 mm) **or** size needed
    for gauge
  Yarn needle

GAUGE: In pattern,
  (dc, ch 1) 7 times (14 sts) = 4" (10 cm)
  Each Strip = 3¹/₂" (9 cm) wide

Gauge Swatch: 3¹/₂"w x 3³/₄"h (9 cm x 9.5 cm)
With Red, ch 14.
Work same as Strip.

Each row is worked across length of Strip. When joining yarn and finishing off, leave a 5¹/₂" (14 cm) end to be worked into fringe.

STITCH GUIDE
BOBBLE
Ch 3, sc in second ch from hook, (2 dc, sc) in last ch. Fold Bobble with first sc on top of last sc and slip st in first ch.
ANCHOR SC
Insert hook in top 2 loops of next ch **and** in top loop of center ch of ch-5 one row **below**, YO and pull up a loop, YO and draw through both on hook.

STRIP (Make 10)
FIRST HALF
With Red, ch 170.

Row 1 (Right side): Sc in second ch from hook and in next ch, work Bobble, ★ skip next ch, sc in next ch, ch 1, skip next ch, sc in next ch, work Bobble; repeat from ★ across to last 3 chs, skip next ch, sc in last 2 chs: 42 Bobbles, 86 sc, and 41 ch-1 sps.

Note: Loop a short piece of yarn around last Bobble made on Row 1 to mark **right** side and **top** edge.

Row 2: Ch 1, turn; keeping Bobbles to **right** side, sc in first 2 sc, ch 1, (sc in next sc, ch 1) across to last 2 sc, sc in last 2 sc: 86 sc and 83 ch-1 sps.

Row 3: Ch 4 **(counts as first dc plus ch 1)**, turn; (dc in next ch-1 sp, ch 1) across to last 2 sc, skip next sc, dc in last sc; finish off: 85 dc and 84 ch-1 sps.

Row 4: With **wrong** side facing, join Ecru with sc in first dc *(see Joining With Sc, page 25)*; ★ ch 5, skip next dc, sc in next dc; repeat from ★ across; finish off: 43 sc and 42 ch-5 sps.

Row 5: With **right** side facing, join Red with sc in first sc; ★ working **behind** next ch-5 *(Fig. 3, page 25)*, (dc, ch 1, dc) in skipped dc one row **below**, sc in next sc; repeat from ★ across: 127 sts and 42 chs.

Row 6: Ch 1, turn; sc in first sc, ch 1, skip next dc, work Anchor sc, ch 1, skip next dc, sc in next sc, ★ ch 1, skip next dc, work Anchor sc, ch 1, skip next dc, sc in next sc; repeat from ★ across; finish off: 85 sc and 84 ch-1 sps.

SECOND HALF
Row 1: With **right** side facing and working in sps and in free loops across beginning ch *(Fig. 2b, page 25)*, join Red with dc in first ch *(see Joining With Dc, page 25)*; ch 1, (dc in next sp, ch 1) across, skip next ch, dc in ch at base of last sc; finish off: 85 dc and 84 ch-1 sps.

Rows 2-4: Repeat Rows 4-6 of First Half: 85 sc and 84 ch-1 sps.

ASSEMBLY
With Red, holding marked ends of Strips at same end and matching sts, whipstitch Strips together through **both** loops *(Fig. 4a, page 25)*, beginning in first sc and ending in last sc.

TRIM
With **right** side facing, join Red with slip st in first sc; (slip st in next ch-1 sp, ch 1) across to last ch-1 sp, slip st in last ch-1 sp and in last sc; finish off.

Repeat across opposite side.

Using photo as a guide for placement and holding 2 strands of corresponding color yarn together, each $11^{1}/_{2}$" (29 cm) long, add additional fringe across short edges of Lap Robe *(Figs. 5a & b, page 26)*.

SLIPPERS
■■■□ INTERMEDIATE

Finished Sole Length:

Small	Medium	Large
9" (23 cm)	$9^{1}/_{2}$" (24 cm)	10" (25.5 cm)

Size Note: Yarn amounts and gauge are given for size Small with sizes Medium and Large in braces { }. Follow the same instructions for **all** sizes. Finished measurement is obtained by using a different hook size as recommended in Materials.

MATERIALS
Medium/Worsted Weight Yarn (4 MEDIUM)
[6 ounces, 330 yards
(170 grams, 300 meters) per skein]:
Ecru - 1 skein
Red - 1 skein
Crochet hook as indicated below **or** size needed for gauge
Size Small: size G (4 mm)
Size Medium: size H (5 mm)
Size Large: size I (5.5 mm)
Safety pin
Marker
Yarn needle

GAUGE: In pattern, 15{14-13} sts and 16{15-14} rows = 4" (10 cm)

Gauge Swatch: 4" (10 cm) square
With Ecru, ch 16{15-14}.
Row 1: Sc in second ch from hook and in each ch across: 15{14-13} sts.
Rows 2 thru 16{15-14}: Ch 1, turn; sc in each sc across.
Finish off.

Instructions begin on page 21.

STITCH GUIDE

RIGHT DECREASE (uses next 2 sts)
Pull up a loop in next sc, YO, working **behind** next ch, insert hook in skipped st one rnd **below**, YO and pull up a loop, YO and draw through 2 loops on hook, YO and draw through all 3 loops on hook.

LEFT DECREASE (uses next 2 sts)
YO, working **behind** next ch, insert hook in skipped st one rnd **below**, YO and pull up a loop, YO and draw through 2 loops on hook, pull up a loop in next sc, YO and draw through all 3 loops on hook.

SOLE

With Ecru, ch 24.

Rnd 1 (Right side)**:** 2 Sc in second ch from hook, sc in next 9 chs, hdc in next 3 chs, dc in next 7 chs, 2 dc in next ch, hdc in next ch, 5 sc in last ch (toe); working in free loops of beginning ch *(Fig. 2b, page 25)*, hdc in next ch, 2 dc in next ch, dc in next 7 chs, hdc in next 3 chs, sc in next 9 chs, 2 sc in same ch as first sc; do **not** join, place marker *(see Markers, page 24)*: 53 sts.

Note: Loop a short piece of yarn around any stitch to mark Rnd 1 as **right** side.

Rnd 2: 2 Sc in each of next 2 sc, sc in next 22 sts, 2 sc in next sc, (sc in next sc, 2 sc in next sc) twice, sc in next 22 sts, 2 sc in each of next 2 sc: 60 sc.

Rnd 3: Sc in next sc, 2 sc in next sc, sc in next 23 sc, 2 sc in next sc, (sc in next 2 sc, 2 sc in next sc) 3 times, sc in next 23 sc, 2 sc in next sc, sc in next sc: 66 sc.

Rnd 4: Sc in next sc, 2 sc in next sc, sc in next 26 sc, 2 sc in next sc, (sc in next 2 sc, 2 sc in next sc) 3 times, sc in next 26 sc, 2 sc in next sc, sc in next sc: 72 sc.

Rnd 5: Sc in next 33 sc, 2 sc in next sc, sc in next 4 sc, 2 sc in next sc, sc in next 33 sc; do **not** finish off: 74 sc.

SIDES

Rnd 1: Sc in each sc around; slip st in next sc to join, remove marker and place loop from hook onto safety pin to keep piece from unraveling as you work the next rnd.

Always keep safety pin and working yarn on **wrong** side of work.

Rnd 2: With **wrong** side facing, join Red with sc in sc before joining *(see Joining With Sc, page 25)*; ch 1, skip next sc, ★ sc in next sc, ch 1, skip next sc; repeat from ★ around; join with slip st to first sc, finish off: 37 sc and 37 chs.

Rnd 3: With **right** side facing, remove safety pin and place Ecru loop onto hook; ch 3 **(counts as first dc, now and throughout)**, sc in next sc, ★ working **behind** next ch *(Fig. 3, page 25)*, dc in skipped st one rnd **below**, sc in next sc; repeat from ★ around; join with slip st to first dc, place loop from hook onto safety pin to keep piece from unraveling as you work the next rnd: 74 sts.

Rnd 4: With **wrong** side facing, join Red with sc in sc before joining; ch 1, skip next st, ★ sc in next sc, ch 1, skip next st; repeat from ★ around; join with slip st to first sc, finish off: 37 sc and 37 chs.

Rnd 5: With **right** side facing, remove safety pin and place Ecru loop onto hook; ch 3, (sc in next sc, working **behind** next ch, dc in skipped dc one rnd **below**) 13 times, (sc in next sc, work Left decrease, working **behind** next ch, dc in skipped st one rnd **below**) 3 times, work Right decrease, sc in next sc, (working **behind** next ch, dc in skipped dc one rnd **below**, work Right decrease, sc in next sc) twice, (working **behind** next ch, dc in skipped dc one rnd **below**, sc in next sc) 12 times; join with slip st to first dc, place loop onto safety pin to keep piece from unraveling as you work the next rnd: 68 sts.

Rnd 6: Repeat Rnd 4: 34 sc and 34 chs.

Rnd 7: With **right** side facing, remove safety pin and place Ecru loop onto hook; ch 3, (sc in next sc, working **behind** next ch, dc in skipped dc one rnd **below**) 12 times, work Right decrease, sc in next sc, (working **behind** next ch, dc in skipped st one rnd **below** ch, work Right decrease, sc in next sc) twice, work Left decrease, (working **behind** next ch, dc in skipped st one rnd **below**, sc in next sc, work Left decrease) twice, (working **behind** next ch, dc in skipped dc one rnd **below** ch, sc in next sc) 11 times; join with slip st to first dc, place loop from hook onto safety pin to keep piece from unraveling as you work the next rnd: 62 sts.

Rnd 8: Repeat Rnd 4: 31 sc and 31 chs.

Rnd 9: With **right** side facing, remove safety pin and place Ecru loop onto hook; ch 3, (sc in next sc, working **behind** next ch, dc in skipped dc one rnd **below**) 9 times, place marker in last dc made for st placement, sc in next sc, (working **behind** next ch, dc in skipped st one rnd **below**, sc in next sc) 3 times, work Left decrease, working **behind** next ch, dc in skipped st one rnd **below**, sc in next sc, work Left decrease, (working **behind** next ch, dc in skipped st one rnd **below**, work Right decrease, sc in next sc) twice, (working **behind** next ch, dc in skipped dc one rnd **below**, sc in next sc) 11 times; join with slip st to first dc, finish off: 58 sts.

INSTEP

With **right** side facing, join Red with dc in marked dc *(see Joining With Dc, page 25)*; remove marker, dc in next 3 sts, hdc in next 4 sts, sc in next 3 sts, slip st in next 3 sts, sc in next 3 sts, hdc in next 4 sts, dc in next 4 sts, leave remaining 33 sts unworked; finish off leaving a long end for sewing: 25 sts.

With **right** side facing and using long end, whipstitch Instep sts together through **inside** loops only *(Fig. 4b, page 25)*, beginning in first dc and last dc and ending in center of slip st.

CUFF

Rnd 1: With **right** side facing, join Red with sc first dc on Rnd 9; sc in next 17 sts, dc in same dc as first dc of Instep; working in end of rows on Instep, sc around post of first dc, sc in next joining and around post of next dc, dc in same sc as last dc of Instep; sc in last 15 sts; do **not** join, place marker: 38 sts.

Rnd 2: Slip st in Back Loop Only of each st around *(Fig. 1, page 25)*; slip st in **both** loops of first slip st to join, finish off.

RUFFLES

With **right** side facing, Sole toward you, and starting on Rnd 2 of Sides, join Red with slip st in Back Loop Only of ch at center of heel; ★ † ch 7, slip st in Front Loop Only of same ch, ch 7, [slip st in Back Loop Only of next ch, ch 7, slip st in Front Loop Only of same ch, ch 7] around †, skip next rnd above, slip st in Back Loop Only of ch above joining slip st; repeat from ★ 2 times **more**, then repeat from † to † once; working in Front Loops Only of Rnd 1 of Cuff and Instep, slip st in first sc, ch 7, (slip st in next st, ch 7) around first half of Cuff, and seam of Instep, then around second half of Cuff; join with slip st to **both** loops of first slip st on Rnd 1 of Cuff, finish off.

YARN INFORMATION

Each project in this leaflet was made with Medium/Worsted Weight Yarn. Any brand of Medium/Worsted Weight Yarn may be used. It is best to refer to the yardage/meters when determining how many balls or skeins to purchase. Remember, to arrive at the finished size, it is the GAUGE/TENSION that is important, not the brand of yarn.

For your convenience, listed below are the specific yarns used to create our photography models.

1. GLOBETROTTER SLIPPERS & THROW
Red Heart® Super Saver®
Red - #319 Cherry Red
Red Heart® Classic®
Purple - #584 Lavender

2. DESERT SUNSET SLIPPERS & THROW
Red Heart® Classic®
White - #1 White
Yellow - #230 Yellow
Orange - #253 Tangerine
Red - #902 Jockey Red
Purple - #596 Purple
Blue - #849 Olympic Blue
Green - #676 Emerald

3. DREAMY SLIPPERS & THROW
Red Heart® Kids
Pink - #2734 Pink
Green - #2652 Lime

4. LEISURE TIME SLIPPERS & THROW
Unger® Utopia
Ecru - #35 Natural
Blue - #120 Bright Blue
Brown - #73 Brown

5. SOOTHING SLIPPERS & THROW
Red Heart® Fiesta
Red - #6915 Burgundy
Ecru - #6013 Wheat

GENERAL INSTRUCTIONS

ABBREVIATIONS

ch(s)	chain(s)
cm	centimeters
dc	double crochet(s)
hdc	half double crochet(s)
mm	millimeters
Rnd(s)	Round(s)
sc	single crochet(s)
sp(s)	space(s)
st(s)	stitch(es)
YO	yarn over

★ — work instructions following ★ as many **more** times as indicated in addition to the first time.

† to † — work all instructions from first † to second † **as many** times as specified.

( ) or [ ] — work enclosed instructions **as many** times as specified by the number immediately following **or** work all enclosed instructions in the stitch or space indicated **or** contains explanatory remarks.

colon (:) — the number(s) given after a colon at the end of a row or round denote(s) the number of stitches or spaces you should have on that row or round.

GAUGE

Exact gauge is **essential** for proper size and fit. Before beginning your project, make the sample swatch given in the individual instructions in the yarn and hook specified. After completing the swatch, measure it, counting your stitches and rows or rounds carefully. If your swatch is larger or smaller than specified, **make another, changing hook size to get the correct gauge**. Keep trying until you find the size hook that will give you the specified gauge.

MARKERS

Markers are used to help distinguish the beginning of each round being worked. Place a 2" (5 cm) scrap piece of yarn before the first stitch of each round, moving marker after each round is complete.

CROCHET TERMINOLOGY

UNITED STATES		INTERNATIONAL
slip stitch (slip st)	=	single crochet (sc)
single crochet (sc)	=	double crochet (dc)
half double crochet (hdc)	=	half treble crochet (htr)
double crochet (dc)	=	treble crochet (tr)
treble crochet (tr)	=	double treble crochet (dtr)
double treble crochet (dtr)	=	triple treble crochet (ttr)
triple treble crochet (tr tr)	=	quadruple treble crochet (qtr)
skip	=	miss

Yarn Weight Symbol & Names	SUPER FINE 1	FINE 2	LIGHT 3	MEDIUM 4	BULKY 5	SUPER BULKY 6
Type of Yarns in Category	Sock, Fingering Baby	Sport, Baby	DK, Light Worsted	Worsted, Afghan, Aran	Chunky, Craft, Rug	Bulky, Roving
Crochet Gauge Ranges in Single Crochet to 4" (10 cm)	21-32 sts	16-20 sts	12-17 sts	11-14 sts	8-11 sts	5-9 sts
Advised Hook Size Range	B-1 to E-4	E-4 to 7	7 to I-9	I-9 to K-10.5	K-10.5 to M-13	M-13 and larger

ALUMINUM CROCHET HOOKS

U.S.	B-1	C-2	D-3	E-4	F-5	G-6	H-8	I-9	J-10	K-10½	N	P	Q
Metric - mm	2.25	2.75	3.25	3.5	3.75	4	5	5.5	6	6.5	9	10	15

■□□□ BEGINNER		Projects for first-time crocheters using basic stitches. Minimal shaping.
■■□□ EASY		Projects using yarn with basic stitches, repetitive stitch patterns, simple color changes, and simple shaping and finishing.
■■■□ INTERMEDIATE		Projects using a variety of techniques, such as basic lace patterns or color patterns, mid-level shaping and finishing.
■■■■ EXPERIENCED		Projects with intricate stitch patterns, techniques and dimension, such as non-repeating patterns, multi-color techniques, fine threads, small hooks, detailed shaping and refined finishing.

JOINING WITH SC

When instructed to join with sc, begin with a slip knot on hook. Insert hook in stitch or space indicated, YO and pull up a loop, YO and draw through both loops on hook.

JOINING WITH DC

When instructed to join with dc, begin with a slip knot on hook. YO, holding loop on hook, insert hook in stitch or space indicated, YO and pull up a loop (3 loops on hook), (YO and draw through 2 loops on hook) twice.

BACK OR FRONT LOOP ONLY

Work only in loop(s) indicated by arrow *(Fig. 1)*.

Fig. 1

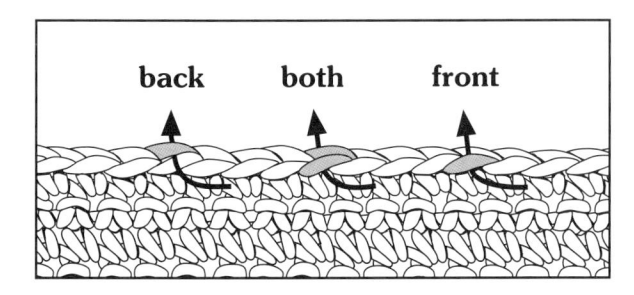

FREE LOOPS

After working in Back or Front Loops Only on a row or round, there will be a ridge of unused loops. These are called the free loops. Later, when instructed to work in the free loops of the same row or round, work in these loops *(Fig. 2a)*.

When instructed to work in free loops of a chain, work in loop indicated by arrow *(Fig. 2b)*.

Fig. 2a   **Fig. 2b**

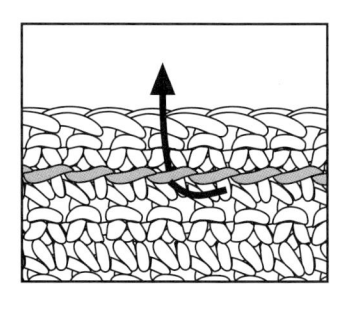

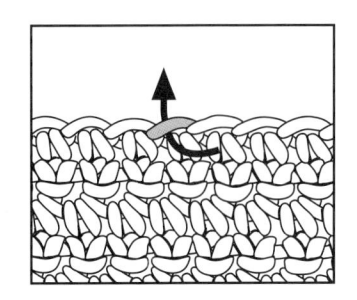

WORKING IN FRONT OF OR BEHIND A STITCH

Work in stitch or space indicated, inserting hook in direction of arrow *(Fig. 3)*.

Fig. 3

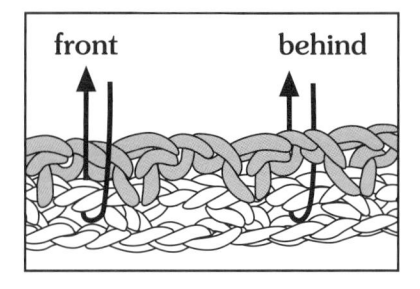

WHIPSTITCH

With **wrong** sides together and beginning in stitch indicated, sew through **both** pieces once to secure the beginning of the seam, leaving an ample yarn end to weave in later. Insert the needle from **front** to **back** through **both** loops on **each** piece *(Fig. 4a)* **or** through **inside** loops *(Fig. 4b)*. Bring the needle around and insert it from **front** to **back** through next loops of both pieces. Continue in this manner across, keeping the sewing yarn fairly loose.

Fig. 4a   **Fig. 4b**

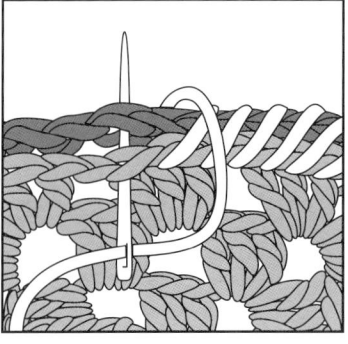

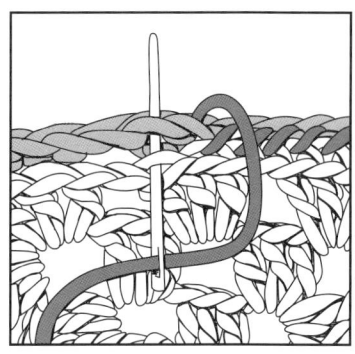